Collecting

BLACK MEMORABILIA

A PICTURE PRICE GUIDE

by

J. P. Thompson

Published by

L-W Book Sales
P.O. Box 69
Gas City, IN 46933

ISBN#: 0-89538-077-3

Published by: L-W Book Sales
P.O. Box 69
Gas City, IN 46933

Please write for our free catalog.

Printed by IMAGE GRAPHICS, INC., Paducah, Kentucky

TABLE OF CONTENTS

INTRODUCTION

Collecting continues to be a favored recreation for many people, with new collectors entering the market everyday. It is usually a good idea to collect the things you like to see around you, rather than collect only the pieces you think will increase in value.

Prices vary from coast to coast and shop and flea market prices differ from auction prices. Prices are also affected by availability and condition.

Prices listed in this book are for items in good condition. Prices listed should be used as a guide only. Any losses that may occur from consulting this book are not the responsibility of the publisher or author.

DEDICATON

This book is dedicated to A. J. Thompson for his help and encouragement. With special thanks to R. & H. Prisby, P. D. Prisby, H. & L. Smith, R. R. Prisby III & L. Raines for their encouragement.

DISPLAYING YOUR COLLECTIBLES

When displaying a large number of small pieces, consider grouping them by color or category. Mix pieces with varying heights to give your grouping interest. Small boxes, (empty wax paper and match boxes), books and other containers can be used to create varying heights. Boxes can be covered with fabric or simply draped with cloth napkins, handkerchiefs, or doilies, old or new.

Use bookcases, display cases or even stacked wooden fruit crates to house your collectibles. Resist the temptation to cover a lot of flat surfaces, (tables, dressers, buffets,) with small pieces.

If your collection is truly a large one consider keeping the major portion in one area or room and carefully incorporate pieces from your collection with the decorating scheme throughout your home. You can change these pieces every few months or so if you like.

If you plan to decorate a room with many small pieces, pictures, wall hangings, etc. keep wall, curtain and floor covering patterns simple. The more you plan to put in a room, especially small things, the less busy the background should be. Treat the background as a blank canvas to showcase your collectibles.

Have fun collecting.
J.P. Thompson

DISPLAYING YOUR COLLECTION

Items on this page are priced throughout the book.

Bottom left:
Salt & Pepper Set with the blue and green lids, are 2¾".
$40-50

Other items on this page are priced throughout the book.

DISPLAYING YOUR COLLECTION

Top Row:
A six piece Spice Set by F. & F. Mold and Die,
Dayton, Ohio, 1949, hard plastic, no rack, 4" tall.
$300-400

Bottom Row:
Two pairs of Salt and Pepper Shakers, 3".
$35-50 a pair

Left and Right:
Two Yarn Bell Dolls, 5 1/2" tall.
$25-35 each

Middle:
Cast Iron Bank, 7 3/4" tall.
(if original) – **$185**
(reproduction) – **$15-25**

Left and Right:
Two Bisque Nodder Banks, 6" tall, Japan.
$40-65 each

Middle:
Gollywog Perfume Bottle, 3" tall, France.
$110-160

DISPLAYING YOUR COLLECTION

Middle:
Aunt Jemima Cookie Jar, hard plastic, 12", by F. & F. Mold and Die, Dayton, Ohio.
$350-450

Front:
Two Male Salt Shakers with red jackets and yellow pants, 3½" tall, by F. & F. Mold and Die, Dayton, Ohio.
(if paired with female mates) – **$40-45 a pair**

Sides:
Five Aunt Jemima Syrup Pitchers, 5½" tall, by F. & F. Mold and Die, Dayton, Ohio.
$55-70 each

Wall Hangings:
2 Cream of Wheat Prints – **$35-65 each**

Middle & Bottom of Shelf:
3 sets of large Salt and Pepper Shakers, 5" tall – **$45-50 each set**

Both Ends of Shelf:
2 sets of Aunt Jemima Cream and Sugar sets, by F. & F. Mold and Die, Dayton, Ohio – **$150-185 set**

Left:
Appliance Cover Doll – **$65-80**

Middle (left to right):
Lg. 3-lb. Luzianne Tin – **$200-230**
Sm. 1-lb Luzianne Tin – **$95-130**
Head Planter, 5" tall – **$40-90**

Right:
Cookie Jar, 12" tall, by F. & F. Mold and Die – **$350-450**

Salt and Pepper, 5" tall, by F. & F. Mold and Die – **$40-50**

DISPLAYING YOUR COLLECTION

Left to Right:
Cloth Stuffed Doll, 15" tall – **$35-45**
Advertising Tin, 8 1/4" – **$35-65**
Advertising Tin, 10 1/2" – **$40-80**
Small stuffed doll, 9" tall – **$50-70**

Left to Right:
Hard Plastic Doll, 8" tall – **$25-30**

Chalk Male Figure, top of a tobacco
humidor, 5" tall – **$50-95**

Appliance Cover Doll – **$45-80**

Top Row:
2 Appliance Cover Dolls – **$55-95**

Bottom Row:
Composition Doll, 9 1/2" tall – **$85-95**

DISPLAYING YOUR COLLECTION

Left and Right Sides:
2 Sets of Salt and Pepper Shakers, ceramic, small set is 3" tall – **$35-40**
large set is 4" tall – **$45-50**

Middle:
Head Vase, female, ceramic, 5" tall – **$40-80**

Left and Right Sides:
2 Sets of Salt and Pepper Shakers, 3" tall, Japan – **$25-35**

Middle:
Cast Iron Soap Dish, lady with a basket on her head, 51/4" tall – **$300-450**

Left and Right Sides:
2 Female wooden brooms, 7" tall.
$40-55 each

Middle:
Flat Doll, wooden, 13" tall.
$75-125

DISPLAYING YOUR COLLECTION

Left:
Female Spoon Holder, chalkware,
5¾" tall – **$50-75**

Right:
Salt and Pepper Shaker Set,
ceramic, 4½" tall.
$60-65 pair

Left:
Boy on an Elephant ceramic Salt
and Pepper Shaker Set, 5½" tall,
Japan – **$100-150 a set**

Right:
Salt Shaker with the identical
mate missing, 5" tall, Japan.
$65-85 each

Back Row:
Sides: 2 Elephant Teapots, 6" x 6½", Japan – **$90-125**   Middle: Camel Teapot, 8" x 9", Japan – **$150-200**

Front Row:
Left: Native on Elephant, 2¼" – **$35-45**   Right: Native on a Blue Elephant, 3", Japan – **$35-50**

DISPLAYING YOUR COLLECTION

Items on this page are priced throughout the book.

DISPLAYING YOUR COLLECTION

In the Basket:

A large stuffed doll with ribbons in her hair, 18" tall – **$30-50**

4 Piece Doll Set including: Aunt Jemima, Uncle Moses, Diane and Wade,
stuffed oil cloth dolls from 9" tall to 12" tall – **$275-375 set**

Left to Right on Floor:

Boy with Watermelon Ceramic Bank, 12" tall – **$125-175**

2 Yellow Luter's Pure Lard Tins, 4lbs. – **$100-150 each**

White Luzianne Coffee Sample tin, 5½" tall – **$95-135**

Concrete Fisher Boy, 14" tall – **$35-45**

DISPLAYING YOUR COLLECTION

Top Shelf:
Left and Right side: An Aunt Jemima creamer and sugar, yellow plastic, by F. & F. Mold and Die – **$150-185 set**

Middle: A Salt and Pepper Set, 5 3/4", made in U.S.A. – **$60-100 set**

Bottom Shelf:
Left and Right side: A Salt and Pepper Set marked "Salty" and "Peppy", 7 3/4" tall, Pearl China – **$150-250 pair**

Identical smaller set to the set above marked Salty & Peppy, 4 1/2" – **$85-150 pair**

2 Pairs of Salt and Pepper Shakers, made in U.S.A., 4 3/4" tall – **$45-60 pair**

Middle: Pot Holder, 5" – **$25-35**

Middle of Shelf:
Pearl China Female Cookie Jar, 11" tall.
$800-950

Pearl China Male Cookie Jar, 10" tall.
$500-700

Front of Mantle:
Porter Tie Rack, pressed wood, 7 1/2" x 8 1/2",
metal rods missing.
$75-100

*Other items on this page are priced
throughout the book.*

DISPLAYING YOUR COLLECTION

Left to Right:

Bisque Male Figure Sitting, 4" tall.
$35-65

Hard Plastic Doll in yellow and white, 61/4" – **$25-35**

Yellow Appliance Cover Doll, with a red head scarf – **$35-85**

Top:
Child with Umbrella Wall Plaque, chalk, 8".
$50-65

Top Left:
Toaster Cover Doll in a yellow checked dress.
$55-85

Top Right:
Male and Female Salt and Pepper Set with square stove, sugar or grease container, 41/2".
$150-250 – 3 piece set

Male Bisque figure sitting, 4" – **$35-65**

Bottom:
Male and Female Banks, cast iron, 41/2" tall.
if original – **$125-150 each**
if reproductions – **$10-20 each**

Apple Doll with bonnett. – **$20-30**

DISPLAYING YOUR COLLECTION

Left to Right:

Stuffed Doll on a papier-mache Donkey, painted face, wire covered body, 6" tall – **$15-20**

Clay Doll with Flag, 7" tall – N.P.A.

Cloth Doll sitting with a basket, 4" tall – **$15-25**

Lady with Basket on head, 7" tall – **$20-35**

Hand carved wooden Male Figure, 7½" tall, with a mohair wig – **$35-65**

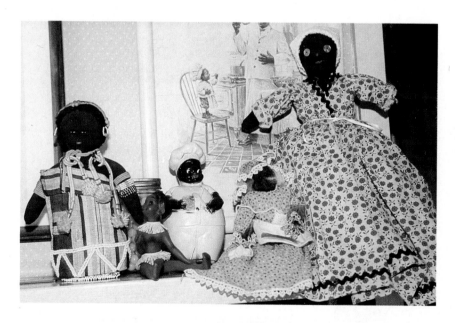

Left to Right:

Cloth Stuffed Doll, 5" x 9½", stitched features – **$85-150**

Bisque Female, 4½" tall, Germany – **$50-85**

Chalk String Holder, 7½" tall – **$90-125**

Apple Doll, 8" tall – **$25-35**

Appliance Cover Doll – **$50-85**

DISPLAYING YOUR COLLECTION

Salt and Pepper Set with a grease or
sugar container, 3 pieces.
$150-250

Child with Watermelon container, 4³/₄".
$60-85

Left to Right:
Ceramic Salt and Pepper Set, a man's head
and a watermelon, 2¹/₄" tall.
$40-60 set

Doll by Shoenhut Toy Co., wooden, 9" tall,
redressed, original hat.
if all original – **$495**

DISPLAYING YOUR COLLECTION

Top Row:
6 Piece Ceramic Spice Set in original rack, 3 1/4" tall, Japan.
$125-170

Bottom Row:
Celluloid doll, 2 3/4" tall – **$25-35**

Child on tray with dice, all celluloid, 1 1/2" x 2 1/2" – **$45-75**

Whiskey Decanters with male figures on front, 8 1/2" tall, Japan.
$65-85 each

Top Row:
3 Pieces of a Spice Set (1 piece is missing to complete set), 5" tall, Japan.
$20-30 each piece

Left and Right:
2 Sets of Matching Salt and Pepper Shakers, 3" tall – **$40-45 each set**

Middle:
2 Ceramic Angels, 5 1/4" tall, Japan .
$40-45 each

DISPLAYING YOUR COLLECTION

Left to Right:
Porter, pot metal, 3" tall – **$35-75**

2 Composition Porters, 3¼" tall.
$25-40 each

Cloth Stuffed Doll, 34" tall, redressed – **N.P.A.**

Left and Right Side:
Salt and Pepper Set, 5" tall,
U.S.A. – **$30-60**

Middle:
Salt Shaker by F. & F. Mold and
Die, 5" tall – **$85-125 each piece**

DISPLAYING YOUR COLLECTION

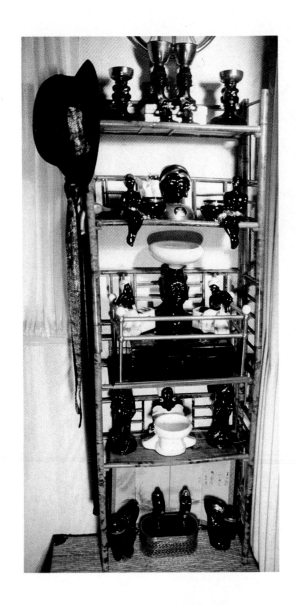

Items in this picture are priced throughout the book.

Left and Right Sides:
2 Female Head Vases, trimmed in gold ceramic, 5 1/2" – **$20-38**

Top Center:
2 Female Head Vases, all metal, 6 1/2" tall.
$25-40 each

Bottom Center:
2 Male Figures with gold trim, ceramic, 3" tall.
$30-45 pair

DISPLAYING YOUR COLLECTION

TOP SHELF
Left and Right Sides:
Male and Female Planters. ceramic, trimmed in gold, 6 1/2" tall – **$20-30 each**

Center:
Head Vase, 4" tall – **$45-75**

SECOND SHELF
Left and Right Sides:
Planters, 5 1/2" x 6 1/2" – **$20-25 each**

Center:
Large Female Head Planter, 10 1/2" tall, the bowl on her head is 7" wide – **$35-55**

THIRD SHELF
Left and Right Sides:
2 Ceramic Figures, 10" tall – **$20-30 each**

Center:
Female Ceramic Figure holding container, 6" x 7" – **$40-65**

BOTTOM SHELF
Left and Right Sides:
Planters, gold trim, 6 1/2" tall – **$20-35 each**

Center:
Salt & Pepper Set, 4" tall, gold trim – **$35-45**

This photo is an enlarged version of the top shelf shown in the above picture.

FIGURAL IMAGES

Ceramic Bust marked "Martin Luther King" on
front of the bottom, 9" x 13½" – **$50-80**

Female Hand Carved Bust, wooden, 8" tall.
$45-90

Left:
Female Bust, 12" tall – **$65-95**

*Figure at the right is same one
as pictured above.*

FIGURAL IMAGES

Female Bisque Figure, 4" tall,
Germany – **$50-65**

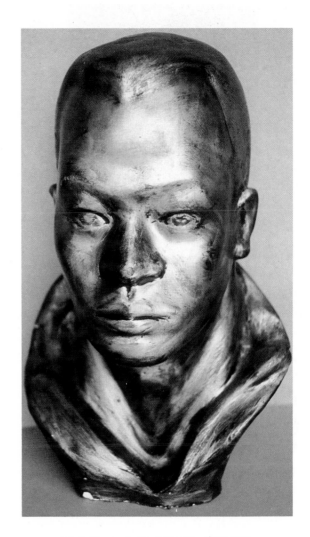

Male Bust, chalk, 16" tall – **$60-100**

2 Female Busts, chalk, 5" tall.
$30-50 each

FIGURAL IMAGES

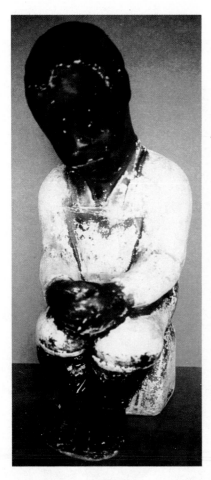

Large Fisher Boy, ceramic, hollow,
8" wide x 19½" tall.
$70-125

Chalk Boy on Potty, 9½" tall – **$40-95**

Flat Wall Hanging, brass on
wood, 10" x 12½".
$45-70

FIGURAL IMAGES

Ceramic Lady with panther, gold trim. The lady is 8" tall, the panther is 10½" long.
$20-35

Ceramic Wall Hanging with gold trim, 8" x 17".
$80-135

Ceramic Male and Female Figures, gold trim, 10" tall.
$20-35 each

FIGURAL IMAGES

Ceramic Male Figure, 8¹⁄₂" tall.
$25-30

Left to Right:
Man Standing wearing bib overalls, Shearwater Pottery, early 1990's, 5" tall.
$60-80

Man Playing an Accordion, Shearwater Pottery, early 1990's, 3" tall.
$50-70

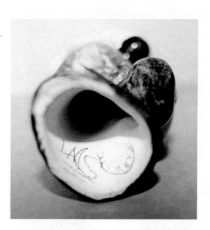

Shearwater Pottery is reproducing new pieces from original molds marked with only the date.
$20-25 each

The original pieces from the early 90's are stamped with the name Shearwater in a circle, as shown this picture.

FIGURAL IMAGES

Ceramic Ladies with textured hair and feather skirts on a base, 4 1/2" tall – **$45-85**

Ceramic Native, textured hair, with animal hair skirt, 4 1/2" tall – **$30-55**

Two Native Ladies Dancing, ceramic, textured hair, animal hair skirts, 4 1/2" tall.   **$30-55 each**

FIGURAL IMAGES

Two Native Men Playing Musical Instruments, ceramic with textured hair and animal hair skirts, 5 1/2" tall.
$35-65

Two Male Native Figures holding drums. Made of ceramic with textured hair, 4 1/2" tall, Japan, marked "Cleveland, Ohio".
$35-65 each

Two Male Native Figures with textured hair, ceramic, one has an animal fur skirt, 4 1/2" tall.
$30-50

FIGURAL IMAGES

Two Ceramic Figures, 3" to 3¼" tall.
$15-25 each

Two Ceramic Figures, 3" to 3½" tall.
$15-25 each

Female Ceramic Figure, textured hair
on a wooden base, 6" tall.
$40-65

Left to Right:
Wooden Letter Opener, 10¾" tall.
$20-35

Brass Letter Opener, 9" tall.
$65-95

FIGURAL IMAGES

Male Figure, gold trim, 3" tall.
$30-45 pair

Metal Book Ends, 3" x 41/2".
$30-50 each

FIGURAL IMAGES

Male Bisque Figures, 2" tall, Japan.
$25-45 each

Three Ceramic Band Players, 4" x 4¾".
$35-65 each

FIGURAL IMAGES

Amos and Andy Ceramic figures,
container, 5 1/2" x 7".
$105-185

Hand Painted Container with gold trim,
5" x 8", Japan.
$200-300

SMOKING ACCESSORIES

Left to Right:
Ceramic Humidor "Amphora", 6" x 6", brass top is missing. Marked "hand painted delft blue Holland" .   **$85-125**

Ceramic Tobacco Humidor, 4" x 41/2". Marked "hand painted delft blue Holland".   **$55-80**

Metal Matchbox Wooden Pull Tray with
gold tipped matches inside, 13/4" x 15/8".
$100-150

SMOKING ACCESSORIES

Left to Right:
Yellow Ashtray with Native laying on the edge,
3 1/4" x 4", Japan. **$30-45**

Round ceramic ashtray, 3" x 6 1/2", Japan – **$20-30**

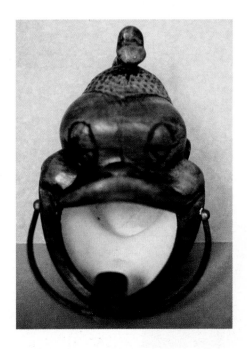

Ceramic Native Head Ashtray, 6 1/2" tall.
$25-35

Metal Alabama Souvenir Ashtray, 4" x 6", Japan.
$30-35

SMOKING ACCESSORIES

Bisque Incense Burner, 4".
$85-125

Native and Alligator Ashtray, ceramic, 4 3/4".
$55-65

Bisque Band Players on a cast iron
ashtray, 2 1/4" x 4".
$125-175

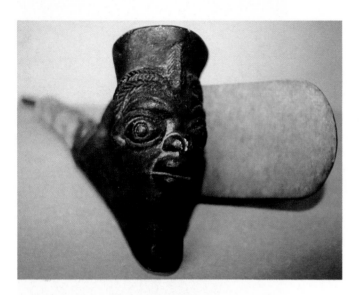

Pipe with a carved bone handle, 12 1/2" long, the face is 5" high.
N.P.A.

This is a close up view of the carved bone handle in above photo.

Wooden Pipe, hand carved, 1 1/2" x 5 1/4".
$125-150

Pipe marked Goedewaagen Gouda Holland, 2" high x 1/2" wide x 5 1/2" long.
N.P.A.

HEAD VASES

Bisque Head Vases, 5 1/2" tall.
$30-38 each

Head Vase Container, ceramic,
10 1/2" tall, the bowl is 7" wide.
$35-55

Left to Right:
2 Head Vases – **$25-35 each**
2 Head Candlestick Holders, gold trim – **$25-35 each**

HEAD VASES

Ceramic Head Vase, 4"
tall with gold trim.
$45-70

Head Vases, gold trim,
red lips, 51/2" tall.
$25-35 each

Head Vase Planters, all metal,
61/2" tall.
$25-45 each

HEAD VASES

Female Head Planter, ceramic, 5" tall.
$40-75

Left to Right:
Female Head Planter, 4¹/2" tall, Japan – **$35-65**
Male Head Planter, 5" tall – **$45-75**

PLANTERS, MATCH HOLDERS, and WALL POCKETS

Ceramic Planter with female standing beside it, 41/2" x 5".
$35-65

Native in a canoe, ceramic planter, 51/2" x 7".
$30-60

One Male and one Female Planter, the figures are sitting on the edge of the planters, 51/2" x 61/2".
$15-25 each

PLANTERS, MATCH HOLDERS, and WALL POCKETS

Male and Female Planters, ceramic with gold trim, 6½" tall.
$20-35 each

Female on an Elephant Planter, 7" x 9".
$30-60

Female and Male Planters,
6½" x 7".
$65-95 each

PLANTERS, MATCH HOLDERS, and WALL POCKETS

Left to Right:
Native sitting on the side of a planter, 5" x 61/2".
$30-45

Native Lady Match Holder, 43/4" tall.
$30-35

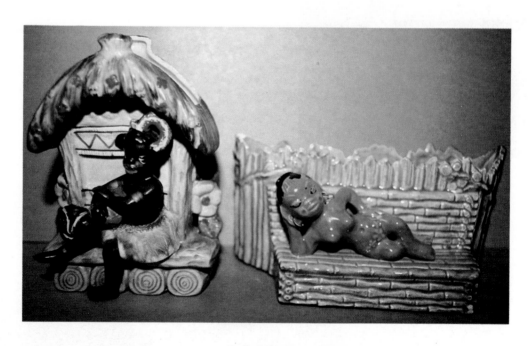

Left to Right:
Native sitting in front of a hut, ceramic planter, 41/2" x 61/2".
$50-85

Native laying on a bench, ceramic planter, 4" x 7".
$35-55

PLANTERS, MATCH HOLDERS, and WALL POCKETS

Female Planter, gold trim, 6 1/2" tall.
$25-35

Male Planter, gold trim, 6 1/2" tall.
$25-35

Male and Female Planters, gold trim, 5 1/2" x 5 1/2".
$60-80 each

PLANTERS, MATCH HOLDERS, and WALL POCKETS

Male and Female Wall Pockets, 6" tall.
$35-65 each

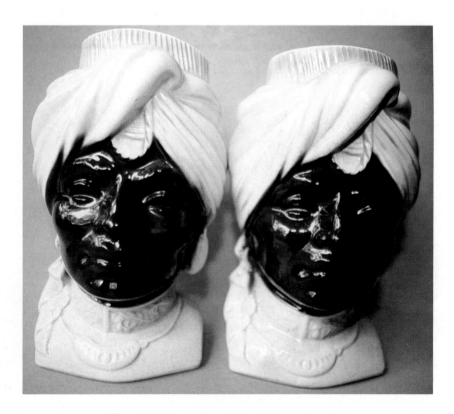

Two Male Head Vases, Royal Copley, 8" tall.
$30-60 each

PLANTERS, MATCH HOLDERS, and WALL POCKETS

Bisque Container, male child, 41/2" tall.
$75-125

Two Planters, one male and one female, ceramic, gold trim, 51/2" x 61/2".
$20-30 each

MORE CONTAINERS

Ceramic Figure with a container
on its head, 31/2" x 4".
$35-55

Ceramic Figure, salt and pepper,
watermelons missing, 4" tall.
$50-75

Lady holding a bowl, ceramic, 6" x 7".
$40-65

MORE CONTAINERS

Jim Beam Limited Edition
"Crispus Attucks" Bicentennial
Bourbon 1976.
$25-38

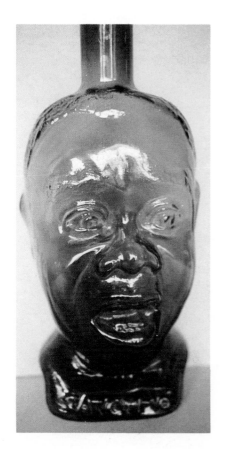

The face of Louis Armstrong, and
"Satchmo" marked on the front,
4 1/2" x 9 1/2".
$40-65

Jim Beam Decanter of John Henry,
by Regal China, 1972, 5" x 13".
$65-90

MORE CONTAINERS

Three Shot Glasses with natives on them, 2 1/4" tall.
$15-20 each

Ice Tea Glasses, 7" tall.
$20-25 each

Ceramic Decanter of a man with a pipe in his
mouth, holding six shot glasses. The hat comes
off to pour, 8" tall, made in Germany.
$175-225

Elephant Decanter, with a removable
trunk, 6 1/2" x 7", Japan.
$45-75

MORE CONTAINERS

Perfume Bottles, later used as
Christmas ornaments, 21/4".
$35-40 each

Salt and Pepper Shaker Set,
gold trim, 61/4" tall.
$35-50

Glass Coasters, 3" tall.
$25-35 each

MORE CONTAINERS

Left:
Salt and Pepper Shakers, 3½", hard plastic. The set at the left is clearly marked on the bottom "by F. & F. Mold & Die, Dayton, Ohio". This set has a green hard plastic stopper in the bottom.
$40-45 pair

Right:
A reproduction set of the ones pictured at the left. The name has been painted over, 3½" tall. This set has a cork stopper in the bottom.
$5-12 set

Ceramic Salt and Pepper Shaker, 2½" and 3½" tall.
$35-40

Man holding a container, gold trim, 7" tall.
$30-50

MORE CONTAINERS

Ceramic Salt and Pepper Shaker Set.
The heads lift off the base, 4" x 5",
Yellowstone Treasure Craft U.S.A.
$35-50

2 Sets of Salt & Pepper Shakers,
ceramic, 3" tall, Japan.
$40-45 each set

Native Salt and Pepper Shaker
set, 4" tall.
$35-45

MORE CONTAINERS

2 Sets of Salt and Pepper
Shakers of Natives, Japan.
Left: 4" tall – **$45-50**
Right: 3" tall – **$35-45**

Salt and Pepper Shaker
Set, 2 1/2" tall, Japan.
$40-60

Wooden Salt and Pepper
Shakers, 4" tall, Japan.
$20-35

MORE CONTAINERS

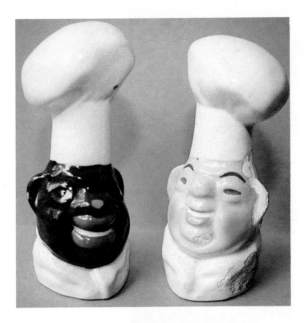

Black and White Chefs, Salt and Pepper Set,
marked Grims California, 41/2" tall.
$60-70

Ceramic Native Mold, 41/2" x 5".
$30-65

Ceramic Pepper Shaker, 3" tall. The
mate bale of cotton is missing.
$45-65 each shaker

Left to Right:
Saucer, Lord Nelsonware, Staffordshire England, newer piece, 41/2" tall.
$30-45

Butter Dish, gold trim, Sandland ware, Staffordshire
England, newer piece, 31/4" x 43/4" tall
$65-110

MORE CONTAINERS

Camel Teapot with a native sitting on top, 6" x 9¼", Japan.
$150-200

Camel Teapot, China, with gold trim, 6" x 9".
Marked "Gold Castle hand painted Chikusa Japan".
$150-200

MORE CONTAINERS

Left and Right Sides:
Salt & Pepper Shaker set, chalk, 21/2" tall.
$45-50

Middle:
Mammy Head Teapot, hard to find, 5" x 51/2".
$500-600

Elephant Teapot with a Native on the lid, 5" x 6".
$45-75

MORE CONTAINERS

Cream and Sugar marked "© C.C. Co. China Co. Wellsville", (hard to find)
The female is 3 1/2" x 6"   The male is 5" x 6"
$150-250 a pair

Creamer, ceramic, with scene of black boy
holding the ducks by a pond, 4" x 4 1/2".
$60-95

Ceramic Creamer, 3 1/2" x 4", Japan.
$85-130

MORE CONTAINERS

Ceramic Chef, 3 piece stacked set, the top is salt and the middle is pepper, and the bottom is a sugar bowl, 3" x 5½".
$100-175+

Ceramic Trivet with serving pieces, (4 pc. set). The trivet is 6" x 6", spoon and fork 8", cake cutter 9".
$100-160

Wooden Coffee Grinder marked "Made in Austria" on label and engraved on metal handle, 4¾" x 8".
$50-95

MORE CONTAINERS

A Female Cookie Jar made by Rick
Wisecarver in 1992, 5½" x 7½".
$45-85

Cookie Jar of a male and female
singing, and the male is playing the
banjo, ceramic, 10" x 11½". Made
by Rick Wisecarver in 1991.
$150-200

MORE CONTAINERS

"Bits of the old south" 8" Plate, by Vernon Kiln.
U.S.A. black workers in the background.
$35-55

Plate 9 1/2" marked "Suriname S.A., right side
Bushnegros.
$10-20

Plate 8 1/4" diameter, marked "Porcelain
Delimoges France" 1973.
$25-35

A Plate by Empire China, pictured is a servant caring for
children.
$30-45

CLOWN PIECES

Clown Grease Pot, marked "grease" on lid, Thames hand painted, 31/3" x 43/4", Japan.
$40-90

Clown Lantern, ceramic and metal, 81/2" tall, Japan.
$60-85

Left to Right:
Clown Salt and Pepper Shaker set, 21/4" x 31/2".
$35-45

Clown Ashtray, ceramic, 5" tall.
$20-30

CLOWN PIECES

Clown Pipes (Ashtrays), ceramic, Japan.
Small: **$20-30**
Large: **$25-35**

Salt and Pepper Shaker Set,
ceramic, 31/2" x 31/2".
$35-55

Salt and Pepper Shaker Set, 3" tall.
$45-50

CLOWN PIECES

Ceramic Tea Set, all marked "Thams Hand Painted Japan".
Creamer: 4" x 5" – **$25-35**
Teapot: 6" x 8" – **$65-105**
Sugar: 4" x 5 1/2" – **$25-35**

Ashtray, 5" tall, ceramic, marked "Thams, Japan".
$35-55

Stacked Tea Set, (3 pieces), marked "Thams, Japan", 9" tall.
$70-110

CLOWN PIECES

Measuring Cups including: 1 cup, 1/2 cup, 1/4 cup, and 1/8 cup.
$50-95 set

Clown Decanter, (cups are missing), with removable hat.
$35-60 if complete

Decanter with Cups, 9" tall and the cups are 1 3/4" tall, with a removable hat.
$50-85

WOODEN PIECES

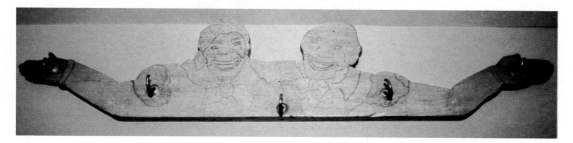

Wooden Folk Art, male and female pot holder rack, 21" long.
$65-95

Tie Rack with a pressed wood male figure, (metal wires missing), 7₁/2" x 8₁/2".
$85-110

WOODEN PIECES

Female Head Cork, 2" tall.
$10-20

Pictured Above and at Left:

Highly polished mahogany Wall Hangings, hand carved, 5" x 8".
$25-45 pair

WOODEN PIECES

Wood and Metal Bottle Openers, a magnet is holding the guitar, 7" tall.
$25-30

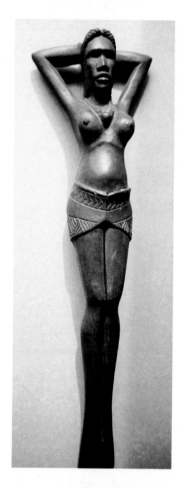

Female Nutcracker,
wooden, 4" x 13".
$25-35

Wooden Ink Pen, celluloid
doll on top, jointed arms,
metal jewelry, mohair wig,
5 3/4" tall.
$35-65

Wooden Pencil,
alligator missing.
$20-30 Pencil only
$40-65 if complete

WOODEN PIECES

Both are hand carved wooden figures, and are 7½" x 22½", wearing red and black outfits. Each is done from a solid block of wood.
$1400-2000 each

Close ups of the Heads from the pieces above.

WOODEN PIECES

Left to Right:
Wooden Folk Art Rattles, the one on the right is marked St. Croix, and has a cloth scarf.
Left: 5 3/4" tall – **$20-30**
Right: 4" x 12" – **$35-75**

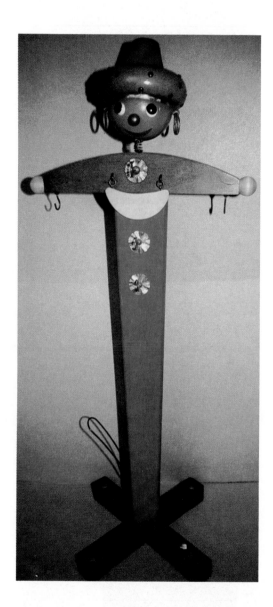

Wooden Figure, 16" x 40", probably used to hang children's clothing on.
$85-120

Flat Wooden Yard Figure, 11" x 14".
$50-85

WOODEN PIECES

Carved Wall Hanging of a child eating a watermelon, 7³/₄" x 9¹/₂", marked R.M. Dion.
$65-95

Wooden Figure used to hold miscellaneous objects 7" x 8".
$25-35

Wooden Wall Hanging, calendar on the front that reads 1937, 5" x 6¹/₂".
$45-65

BANKS, BELLS & BRUSHES

Pressed wood brush holder, of a Porter with Bags, 5" x 7½", brush standing in back.
$50-85

Coconut Head Banks, 5" x 6".
$15-25 each

BANKS, BELLS & BRUSHES

Metal Bell, painted wooden
face, paper skirt, 4" tall.
$25-35

Cast Iron Bank of a Policeman, 8" tall.
$125-195
(watch for reproductions)

Porcelain Bell of a Lady wearing a
long skirt, 3¾" tall, Japan. (The
hands are missing).
$45-50
(if in good condition)

DOLLS

Pot Metal Doll, jointed arms,
painted face, 1 1/2" tall.
$100-150

Cloth Stuffed Doll, 6" tall, with painted facial
features, and string hair.
$20-30

Cloth Stuffed Doll with "Pabst Blue Ribbon"
advertisement around the neck, and has
stitched facial features, and yarn hair.
N.P.A.

DOLLS

Two Dolls, one male one female, 7½" tall, composition, fully jointed, painted faces. The girl has synthetic hair, the boy has molded painted hair, unmarked.
$90-110 each

Hard Plastic Doll, 7½" tall, jointed arms, and a thick mohair wig, and marked on the back of her head "A-7".
$45-65

Composition Doll, 8" tall, painted face, fully jointed, thick synthetic wig, unmarked.
$45-80

DOLLS

Topsy Turvy Doll, with plastic faces, yarn hair, and a cloth stuffed body, 14" tall.
$85-150

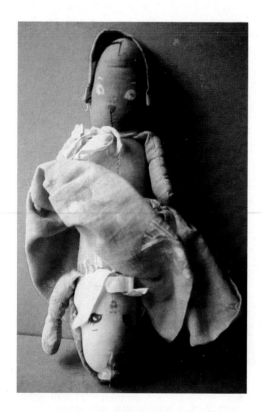

Topsy Turvy Cloth Doll, with a painted face, and yarn hair, 9" tall.
$85-110

Topsy Turvy Cloth Doll, 17" tall, with a full bosom. The black doll has a silk cloth face and arms, satin sleeves, cotton dress and apron. The white doll has heavy cotton face, satin dress, both have stitched features.
$145-200

DOLLS

Topsy Turvy Sock Doll with stitched facial features, (yarn hair has been replaced), newer piece, 14" tall.
$30-50

Topsy Turvy Cloth Stuffed Doll, stitched facial features, newer piece.
$20-30

Topsy Turvy Cloth Stuffed Doll, hard molded face, painted facial features, with swivel heads (and a removable skirt that is missing), 9 1/2" tall.
$100-165

Topsy Turvy Doll, cloth stuffed, painted facial features, 10 1/2" tall.   **$110-150**

DOLLS

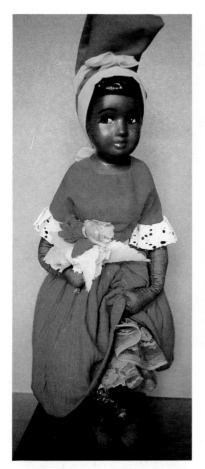

All three island dolls have ceramic heads and shoulders, stuffed bodies, cloth shoes, leather covered legs, molded hair, painted faces, and are sitting on chairs on wooden bases marked "Haiti" on the base, 16" tall.
$110-185 each

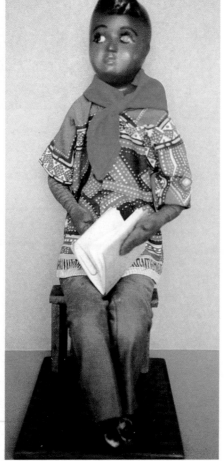

Photo on Right:
This girl with the headscarf is the same as the above dolls, except she has pearl jewelry and is unmarked.

80

DOLLS

Left to Right:
Ceramic Head and Shoulders, cloth stuffed dolls.
9" tall – **$35-55**   11" tall – **$35-65**   11½" – **$45-80**

Ceramic head and shoulder cloth doll, 15" tall.
$55-100

Large ceramic head and shoulders, 6" x 8".
$50-85

DOLLS

Doll with a bisque head and body, jointed composition arms, painted face, thick mohair wig, brass earings, simulated fruit necklace, grass skirt, 6¼" tall.
$95-135

Doll with a ceramic head and shoulders and a cloth stuffed body, molded hair, and 29" tall. The purse that she is carrying has a cloth doll on the front of it. *(all original)*

$350-450+

All Bisque Doll reproduction, bent knees, removable wig, fully jointed. Marked Hilda CJDK 1944 Germany S___gch 1070 or 1970 (marking is unclear), 16" tall.

$90-130

DOLLS

All Bisque Doll wearing a grass skirt, 2" tall.
$45-85

Wooden Nodder Doll, 4" tall, Japan.
$35-65

Reproduction China Doll, 11" tall, cloth body.
$45-60

DOLLS

Fabric Stuffed Doll with a ceramic head and shoulders, 12" tall, with leather covering the legs and standing on a wood base.
$85-100

Stocking Doll with painted facial features on a molded mask face and fastened to a stuffed black stocking. The black stocking body and bottom of the doll (where the legs would be) are one solid piece, 15" tall.

$300-450+

Fabric Stuffed Doll with a ceramic head and shoulders, 12" tall.
$40-80

DOLLS

Celluloid Doll, molded hair, plastic jewelry, and jointed arms, 6 1/2" tall.
$30-50

Celluloid Carnival Doll, jointed arms, cardboard hat, 9 1/2" tall, Japan.
$50-90

Cloth Stuffed Doll with molded face and mohair wig, 12 1/2" tall.
$35-75

DOLLS

Hard Plastic Doll, sleep eyes, 11" tall.
$35-45

Hard Plastic Doll, sleep eyes, 8" tall.
$25-35

Two Rope Dolls from Barbados, 12"
tall, with felt faces, glued features.
$25-35 each

DOLLS

Nut Face Doll with seed eyes
and arms, and a straw outfit,
7" tall.

$35-45

Nut Head Dolls with seed bodies, dresses, eyes and arms, 3 1/2" tall.
$35-55 pair

Painted Walnut Face Doll, wooden body,
arms and legs, jointed arms, mohair wig,
and 9" tall.   **$45-90**

Wooden Doll with a painted face,
jointed arms and legs, marked
"Cari", 9" tall.

$75-130

DOLLS

Celluloid Doll with jointed arms
and legs, painted face, 2 3/4" tall.
$25-40

Three Celluloid Dolls, dressed in straw and burlap with thick synthetic hair,
jointed arms, sleep eyes, with tribal facial markings. The adults are 7 1/4" tall,
the child is 3 1/2" tall.

Adults – **$35-65 each**
Child – **$25-30**

Wind-up Doll, celluloid head and upper
body, with molded hair. Tin arms, legs and
shoes wearing a string skirt. The winding
mechanism in back, 6 1/2" tall.
$75-130

DOLLS

Gourd Doll, painted face, cloth stuffed arms, 11" tall.
$45-85

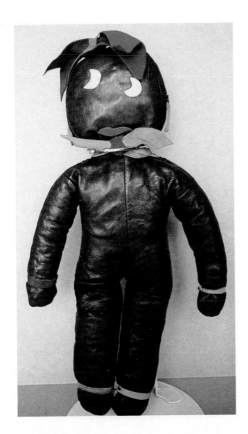

An All Leather Doll, with glued-on facial features, and felt arm bands and leg bands with a bow on its head.
$125-200

Cloth Stuffed Doll with molded painted face and yarn hair, 8" tall.
$35-45

DOLLS

Three hard rubber dolls, molded faces, 6½" tall.
$35-45

Hand Carved Wooden Doll, standing
on a wooden base, mohair wig, and
painted facial features, 7¼" tall.
$35-65

All leather doll with a painted slightly
molded face, 9½" tall.
$25-45

DOLLS

Three sets of Papier Mache Dolls, painted and molded faces, wire covered bodies, and mohair wigs. The males are 6½" tall, and the females are 5" to 6" tall. The bottom set is marked "Cuba".

$55-95 each pair

This set is marked "Cuba"

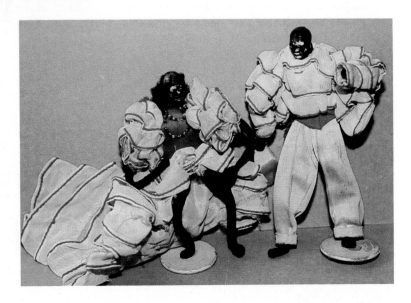

DOLLS

A finely dressed apple faced doll. With a hand crocheted shawl, hat and basket, leather boots, and seed eyes. She has brown leather arms, and metal glasses, 9" tall.
$75-95

Left:
Apple Faced Man Doll, finely dressed in a wool tuxedo, satin lapels, a hat and tie. Wool hair, exceptionally well defined facial features. Wire stuffed arms and legs, wooden shoes, cloth gloves. Beads for the eyes, and a wooden band around the neck, 13" tall.

Right:
A finely dressed female mate, with long crepe 2-piece dress. Hand crocheted front panel and hem of petticoat. Matching crepe fabric hat with feathers. Crepe purse, cloth gloves, wool hair, well defined facial features. Beads for the eyes, wire stuffed arms, and a wooden band around the neck, 11" tall, signed "Etta Austin".

$100-130 each

DOLLS

Two Cloth Stuffed Dolls, hand stitched outfits, stitched facial features, 14" tall.
$100-125 each

Cloth Stuffed Native Doll, flat bottom, finely stitched features, thick yarn hair, bead eyes, elaborate hand beading on arms, hair, neck and top dress, also heavy beadwork on underskirt, 5" x 9½".
$85-150

DOLLS

A finely dressed Apple Doll, in a satin dress, brown leather arms and boots, human hair wig, 9" tall.
$70-95

Apple Faced Doll on a wooden base, wire and cloth stuffed body, cotton wig, dark brown hands, holding a broom, 12" tall.
$35-70

Nora Wellings Doll, velvet head and body, and painted features, 8½" tall.
$95-120

DOLLS

Cloth Stuffed doll, straw hat, painted face,
burlap bag with cotton, 15" tall.
$95-170

Cloth Stuffed Dolls, painted faces,
yarn hair, grass skirts.
left doll: 15" tall – **$85-145**
right doll: 9" tall – **$40-65**.

DOLLS

Velvet Stuffed Doll, molded face, grass skirt by Nora Wellings, 8" tall.
$75-95

Female Stocking, bottle doll, glued felt nose and mouth, 13" tall.
N.P.A.

Velvet Stuffed Doll, molded face, curly mohair wig, glass eyes, tan velvet out-fit, 15" tall.
$250-350

DOLLS

Large cloth stuffed jointed doll, stitched facial features, individually knotted hair, 20" tall.
$90-150

Cloth stuffed doll, 9" tall. With jointed wire covered stuffed arms, mohair around the head, stitched facial features. The doll is holding a broom and a metal dust pan and is standing on a tar paper base.
$90-150

Left to Right:
Wooden jointed dolls.
13" tall – **$75-135**
12" tall – **$45-70**
10" tall – **$30-45**

DOLLS

Cloth stuffed doll, stitched features, fabric hair, beaded eye, and 15" tall.
$90-130

Toaster Cover Stuffed Sock Doll, glued on facial features, 18" to hem.
$45-55

Left to Right:
Cloth doll, thick yarn hair, stitched features, fully jointed, 9" tall. – **$45-80**

Large cloth stuffed doll, molded face, 15" tall – **$35-50**

DOLLS

Appliance Cover Doll, finely stitched
facial features, individually knotted
hair, 18" to hem.
$60-90

3 Appliance Cover Stuffed Dolls, 18" to hem.
$45-85 each

DOLLS

Left to Right:
Three Island Dolls, painted faces, jointed with metal pins in arms and legs, 10" tall, 11" tall, 12" tall.
$50-85

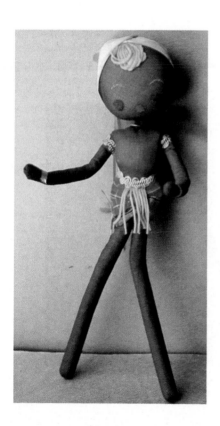

Christmas Ornament, wire covered arms and legs, 7" tall.
$15-25

Large stuffed cloth doll, stitched facial features, individually stitched fingers, thick individually knotted yarn hair, 34" tall, redressed.
N.P.A.

DOLLS

Cloth Stuffed Doll, yarn hair, stitched features, with pearl earrings, and individually stitched fingers, 16" tall.
$85-125

Felt stuffed doll, glued facial features, 11" tall.
$35-50

Stuffed sock doll, button eyes, yarn hair, felt mouth, 17" tall.
$85-130

DOLLS

Left to Right:
Cloth stuffed doll on wooden base, stitched features, 7 1/2" tall.
$15-20

Cloth stuffed Lady on a papier mache donkey, 6" tall.
$15-20

Bottle Stocking Doll, glued on features,
newer, 15" tall.
$30-50

Bottle Doll, plastic face, composition arms and hands, 13" tall.
$35-45

PUPPETS

Wooden Male minstrel puppet, mohair wig, Pelham puppets England, in original box, 13" tall.
$220-300

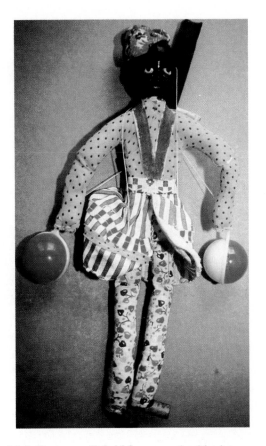

Male Puppet, celluloid face, wooden block torso, wooden shoes, cloth stuffed arms and legs, 13" tall.
$75-85

Female puppet, composition head, arms and legs, 2 wooden blocks for torso, mohair wig, and painted face, 14" tall.   **$250-300**

Male puppet, papier mache head, wooden padded upper and lower body and legs. Leather covered weighted shoes and cloth stuffed arms with yarn hair and a painted face, 20" tall.
$250-400 and up

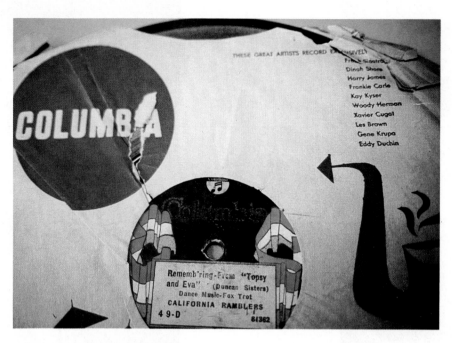

78 Record, "Remembering from Topsy and Eva" by the Duncan Sisters.
Columbia Phonograph Company, with original sleeve, 1909.
$40-65

16mm Headline Edition of Joe Louis-
Baer, Amber-Armstrong, Castle film.
$35-65

78 Record "My Mammy" by Columbia Graphic, Co., 1906-1909 with original sleeve.
$40-60

RECORDS AND FILM

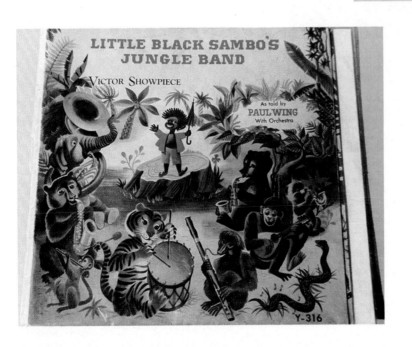

"Spectrum in Black" 1971 poems by 20th Century Poets. Interior with profiles by Romare Bearden.
$20-35

"Little Black Sambo's Jungle Band" Victor Showpiece, record.
Record – **$40-50**
Cover – **$35-45**

"Little Brave Sambo" Peter Pan records narrated by John Bradford and Bobby Hookey 1950.
$45-50

RECORDS AND FILM

78 Columbia Records "Old Black Joe"
Columbia Phonograph, Co., N.Y.,
1913, Tivoli Theater Newark, N.J.,
with original sleeve.
$45-65

78 Columbia Record "Two Black
Crows" part 1 and 2 by Moran and
Mack Columbia phonograph Co., N.Y.,
1913-1923 with original sleeve.
$45-65

Left to Right:
Golden Legacy Magazines

"The saga of Toussaint L'Ouvertur", 1966

"The saga of Harriet Tubman", 1967

"Alexander Dumas and Family, 1967
$10-20 each

BOOKS
All books in frames can be easily removed for viewing.

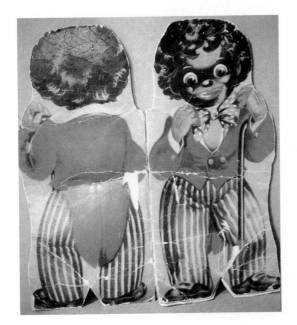 

Golliwog Book, printed in Holland, children's story book, 6" x 13½",
20 pages. No other information is available.
N.P.A.

"Little Black Sambo", 1942, story book by Saalfield Co., Akron, Ohio, 9¾" x 13½". (Framed, but easily removed, illustrated by Ethel Hayes.)
$80-100

"Little Black Sambo", 1942, by Saalfield Publishing Co., 8" x 10½".
$90-110

BOOKS

"Black Pioneers" Booker T. Washington, story by
Lucille Arcola Chambers, the art is by John Neal, C. &
M. Ventures, Inc., NY, 1965, 11" x 18".
$10-25

"The Story of Little Black Sambo" storybook, Junior
Classic illustration by Hildeguard Lupprian,
5¾" x 7½" by McLaughlin Brothers, Inc., © 1931.
$90-125

"Little Black Sambo" book, 5¼" x 6½", by Whitman
Publishing Co., Wisconsin, 1950.
$40-65

BOOKS

"Little Black Sambo" illustrated by Gladys
Turley, Michael Whitman Publishing Co., Wisconsin, 5 1/2" x 6 1/4".
$35-45

"Uncle Tom's Cabin" Young Folks Edition,
Danahugh & Co., 7" x 10".
$85-95

"Uncle Tom's Cabin" Young Folks Edition,
by Harriet Beecher Stowe, 7" x 10".
$85-95

PAPER ADVERTISEMENTS

"The Winner", Joe Louis advertising Chesterfield
Cigarettes, 5" x 6".
$45-75

Kentucky Bob, made in Troupsburg, NY,
Smoking Tobacco Advertisement, 5" x 6".
$45-85

Advertisement for Armour quality product, 1917 Ladies Home Journal.
$50-85

PAPER ADVERTISEMENTS

"Gone are the Good Old Days" advertisement from a magazine for Can Manufacturers Inst. N.Y., Inc., 10 1/2" x 14".
$20-45

1947 Calendar, advertising W. O. Stambaugh Motor Co., 8 1/2" x 14 1/2".
$35-65

A 1928 Proctor & Gamble advertisement from a magazine, "Largest Selling Soap", 14" x 18" .
$20-45

PAPER ADVERTISEMENTS

Advertisement for Sunlight Soap from an illustrated London News, February 8, 1902 by Lever Brothers 11" x 15½".
$75-95

Advertisement for Hiram Walker, Canadian Club, 8" x 11½", 1936 from magazine.
$35-65

A color advertisement for Plantol Soap from the illustrated London News, July 11, 1903, by Lever Brothers, 11" x 15½".
$90-145

Cream of Wheat print by E. Brewer "The For-
tune Teller", from a back cover of a magazine,
linen paper.   **$75-95**

Cream of Wheat print by E. Brewer "That Settles It",
1912, from the back cover of a magazine, linen paper.
$65-95

Cream of Wheat print by E. Brewer "Who can
tell me how to spell Cream of Wheat".
$45-65

Cream of Wheat print by E. Brewer "Jack the Giant Killer",
that reads *Fee! Fi! Fo! Fum! I smell Cream of Wheat Yum-
Yum! Yum-Yum!,* 1909, from the back cover of a magazine,
linen paper.   **$65-75**

PAPER ADVERTISEMENTS

Cream of Wheat Print by E. Brewer
"Giddup Uncle", 1921, linen.
$45-70

Cream of Wheat Print by E. Brewer "A Colored
Supplement", 1916.

$45-70

Cream of Wheat Print by E.
Brewer "Certainement, That's It!
Cream of Wheat!", 1915.
$45-60

PAPER ADVERTISEMENTS

Cream of Wheat Print by E. Brewer
"An Old Friend", 1922.
$35-55

Cream of Wheat Print by E. Brewer "From Sunrise to Twilight".
$35-55

Cream of Wheat Print by E. Brewer
"Starting The New Year", 1923.
$45-65

PAPER ADVERTISEMENTS

Cream of Wheat Print by E. Brewer, "Oh I Done Forgot Dat Cream of Wheat", 1913.
$35-65

Cream of Wheat Print by E. Brewer, "Laying the Cornerstone", 1924.
$35-45

Cream of Wheat Print by E. Brewer "The Connoisseurs", 1916.
$35-65

PAPER ADVERTISEMENTS

Cream of Wheat Print by E. Brewer "Where Healthy Babies Come From", 1922.
$35-45

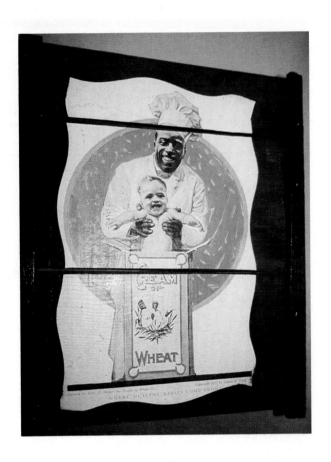

Cream of Wheat Print by E. Brewer "The Blocks Tell The Story".
$35-45

Cream of Wheat Print by E. Brewer "A Dutch Treat", 1915.
$35-60

PAPER ADVERTISEMENTS

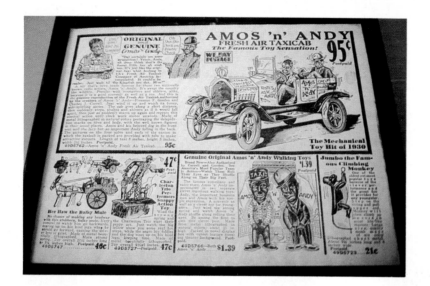

Advertising Print from a magazine
for fresh air taxicab.
$25-35

Six black and white Gold Dust
Twin ads, Fairbanks, Co, 1915.
$30-45

Cream of Wheat Prints from a
magazine, 6" x 8", 1905, black
and white.
$10-15 each

PAPER ADVERTISEMENTS

Two Aunt Jemima Ads, both are from
a 1928 magazine, 101/2" x 14".
$25-35 set

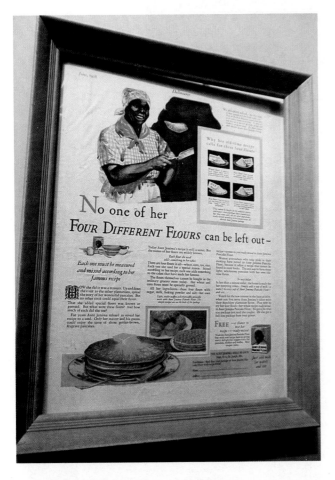

Aunt Jemima Pancake Ad, from a magazine.
$25-45

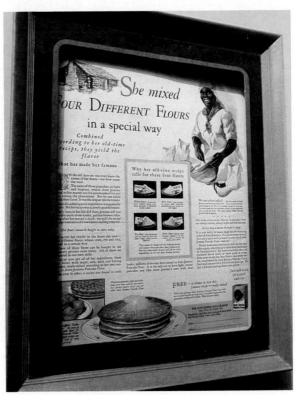

Aunt Jemima Pancake Ad, from a magazine.
$25-45

PAPER ADVERTISEMENTS

Ad for Playing Cards, "Consolidated Card, Co., NY", 8" x 11 3/4".
$85-120
(If in good condition)

Aunt Jemima Ad from a magazine, 10" x 12".
$25-30

Aunt Jemima Ad for Kelloggs Rice Krispies, 1930.
$30-45

PAPER ADVERTISEMENTS

Three Prints, (from a set of six shown on next page), "How To Milk In Fly Time, or Waterberry's Secret", 9" x 10½".
Original set of 6 – **$250-300**
(watch for reproductions)

PAPER ADVERTISEMENTS

Three Prints, (from a set of six shown on previous page), "How To Milk In Fly Time, or Waterberry's Secret", 9" x 10½".
Original set of 6 – **$250-300**
(watch for reproductions)

PAPER ADVERTISEMENTS, TINS, SIGNS & GLASSWARE

Top:
Black Joe Label by Ed Kurtz,
4" x 13". **$25-35**

Bottom:
Aunt Sue's Clothes Cleaner
Advertising Card, Irvington,
NY, 2¾" x 4¾".
$20-35

Cotton Picker Corn Whiskey,
bottled and distilled by Old Quaker
Co., Lawrenceburg, IN, 4" x 8½".
$50-95

Left: Coon Chicken Inn Glasses, 4½";
Mid. & Rgt: Sambo's Bar & Grill, Shot Glasses, 3" tall & 2¼" tall.
$25-35 each

A 1900's Aunt Jemima Breakfast Club
Plate, 11" dia., new design.
$15-25

ADVERTISING TINS, SIGNS AND GLASSWARE

Two Biscuit Tins, with a black butler marked Tendeco.
Left: 10½" – **$40-80**
Right: 8" – **$35-65**

Two pot metal dolls in a wooden box on a leather glove. The box reads "Two Pairs of Undressed Kids", Denver, Colo. The dolls are 1" tall, and the box is 1½" x 3½".

$125-150 pair

Biscuit Tin from the Southern Biscuit Co., that reads "Southern Cakes for Southern Taste", 10" dia.

$100-125

ADVERTISING TINS, SIGNS AND GLASSWARE

Paul Jones, Co., Whiskey Tin, Louisville, KY, 1880's,
flat with folded scroll corners, faded condition, 12 1/2" x 19 1/2".
Mint Condition – **$1200-1400**
Faded Condition – **$200-400**

Budweiser King of Bottled Beer Serving Tray, sheet metal, 13" x 17 1/2".
$160-250

Coconut Cookie Tin, Zombies Co., Miami, Florida.
Left: 6½" wide x 2½" deep – 1/2-lb. – **$20-35**
Right: 6½" wide x 4" deep – 1-lb. – **$30-45**

Zanzibar Brand Ground Mustard Tin with contents,
10 lbs., by B. Heller & Co., 7" x 10¾".
$180-250

Honey Brand Pure Lard Tin, 50 lbs., Packed by Hygrade Food
Products Corp., Detroit, MI, 12½" x 14".
$35-65

Side view of below photo.

Candy Tin, Hollingsworth unusual candies, 31/2" x 73/4".
Marked on front "A peep into the future"
and marked on the side "The spinning wheel".
$85-145

ADVERTISING TINS, SIGNS AND GLASSWARE

Benne Wafer Advertising Tin, 6¼" x 6".
$40-80

(Newer tins were made with the same woman with a white face.)

Benne Bits Advertising Tin, 6¼" x 6".
$40-80

(Newer tins were made with the same woman with a white face.)

Metal Tin, goose chasing a child, 4" x 6".
$85-120

PICTORIAL IMAGES

"Wee Wee Negro Caprice" by
Victor E. Hammerel, 1877
Copyright J. M. Stoddard Co.,
9" x 11".
$45-70

Black and white Print marked "Rebel Negro Pickets As
Seen Through A Field Glass", 6" x 8".
$25-35

Currier and Ives print (reprint) in
1951 for a calendar, published by
The Travelers of Hartford, CT,
11" x 16".
$40-85

PICTORIAL IMAGES

Large Oil Painting on canvas signed
M. Tornello, 23" x 26".
$600+

Pencil Sketch, unsigned, 5 1/2" x 10".
$65-85

Large Oil Painting on pressed
board, signed "Shatter", 21" x 25".
$110-160

PICTORIAL IMAGES

Poker Series Plate #3, "A Rise in the South", copyright 1894 by Truth Co., reprinted in the 1940s by American Litho, Co., NY and Chicago, 16" x 20". This 1940s reprint is framed and matted.
$85-120

Poker Series Plate #4, "A Bluff in Chicago", copyright 1895 by Truth Co., reprinted in the 1940s by American Litho Co., NY and Chicago, 16" x 20". This 1940s reprint is framed and matted.   **$85-120**

PICTORIAL IMAGES

Black and White Print of the Civil War Scene, 20" x 10". "Assault of the Second Louisiana Colored Regiment on the Confederate Works at Port Hudson", May 27, 1863.

$45-65

A black and white print of slaves being sold at auction, 18" x 12", framed and matted.

$45-85

PICTORIAL IMAGES

Picture of Santa with Golliwog Doll
in the sack of toys, from a magazine
or newspaper, 14" x 19½".
$35-45

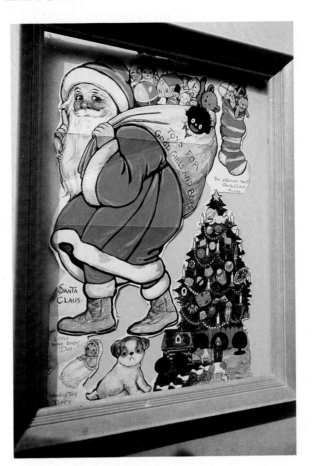

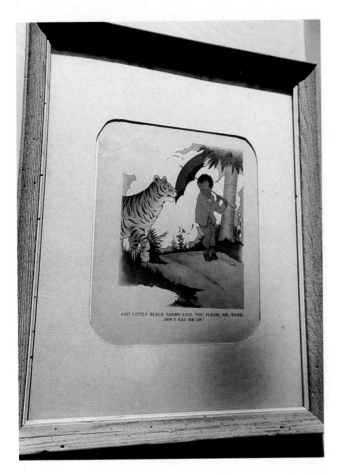

Tiger Stalking Little Black Sambo, 11" x 18".
$45-65

Color print, "True Blue", 16" x 21".
$60-125

(Watch for reproductions)

PICTORIAL IMAGES

1876 Harpers Weekly Print, "The Thanksgiving Turkey", black and white, 15" x 20", framed.
$40-65

Harpers Weekly Cover Print, New York, Dec. 9, 1876. "The Ignorant Vote" framed, 15" x 20".
$45-65

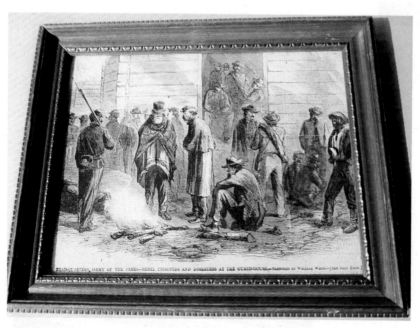

Army Headquarters with rebel prisoners and deserters at the guard house, black and white print, 8" x 10".
$25-30

PICTORIAL IMAGES

A black and white print called "Ignorance is Bliss",
from an original by E. W. Kemball, 11" x 14".
$35-55

Black and White Print from an original sketch by A. B. Frost, 12" x 12".
$35-55

Color Print, 10"x 10".
$35-45

PICTORIAL IMAGES

Print, black and white, "An Authentic Ghost Story", 11" x 9".
$25-30

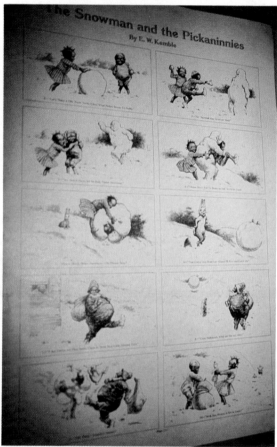

Print from a 1911 Newpaper, "The Snowman and the Pickaninnies" by E. W. Kemble, 11" x 16".
$40-80

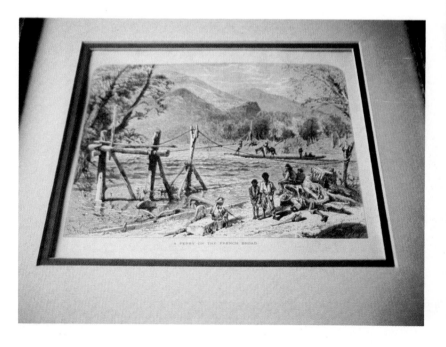

"A Ferry on the French Broad" print, 8" x 10".
$28-30

PICTORIAL IMAGES

An original charcoal and crayon drawing of a man playing a drum, 6½" x 8½".
$80-110

Currier and Ives reprinted in 1951 for a calendar, 11" x 16", called "The Old Barn Floor", by The Travelers of Hartford, CT.
$45-85

PICTORIAL IMAGES

One dollar bills "Dick Gregory for President", 1968, 2½" x 6".
$5-10 each

Card Game, die cut, score pad (behind trunk), a Gibson
Product U.S.A.

$30-45

Halloween Mask, cardboard, 7" x 8¼".
$20-40

PICTORIAL IMAGES

1905 Post Cards, framed.
$12-18 each

Left Photo and Bottom 2 Photos:

6 Post Cards
$8-12 each

PICTORIAL IMAGES

1941 Folding Post Card, "Greetings from Dixieland".
$15-20

1941 Folding Post Card, "Greetings from Dixieland" inside the top of left card.
$15-20

Post Card of St. Augustine, Florida.
$12-18

Old Slave Market Post Card.
$12-18

MUSIC

1933 Stormy Weather, Music Book, 33 pages, 7" x 10¾".
$45-65

Sheet Music, "Five imaginary early Louisiana songs of slavery", 1929, by Shimmer, NY.
$35-65

Sheet Music, "If You Love Your Baby, Make Goo Goo Eyes".
$45-55

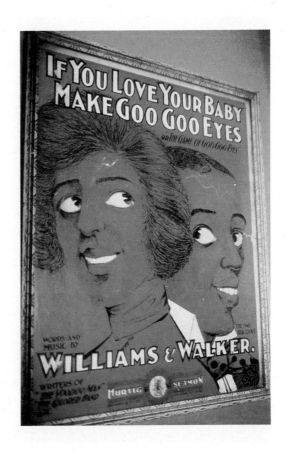

MUSIC

Theater Program, Ethel Waters in "Cabin in the Sky", April 4, 1944, 6 pages.

$35-65

Louis Armstrong 50 Hot Choruses for Cornett, Melrose Bros., 18 pages.

$25-60

Theater Program "Bill Robinson in Hot Mikado", 1939, 6 pages.

$25-60

MUSIC

Sheet Music "Jumbo Jim" by John
Francis Gilder Band Orchestra.
$35-65

Sheet Music, "Short'nin' Bread"
by James Conrad, 1933.
$35-65

Sheet Music, "Dry Bones", piano solo
with words published by Belwin, Inc.,
1949.

$35-65

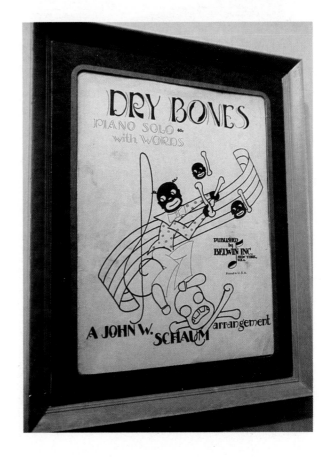

MUSIC

Sheet Music, "What You Going To Do When The Rent Comes Round", 1905.
$35-70

Sheet Music, "Mandy Lane", music by Wm. McKenney.
$35-65

Sheet Music, "If You Want To Keep Your Daddy Home", by Porter Grainger, 1923.
$35-40

MUSIC

Sheet Music, "My Cutey's Due At
Two-To-Two To-day", 1926.
$30-50

Sheet Music, "Praying For The Lights To
Go Out", words and music by Tunnah
and Skidmore.
$35-75

Sheet Music, "Mammy's
Little Coal Black Rose".
$35-40

MUSIC

Sheet Music, "Keep a' knockin'",
music by Frank Pallma, published
by The Brainards Son, Co., 1877.
$45-70

Sheet Music, "There's Something Nice
About Everyone, But There's Everything
Nice About You", by Henry Waterson, Inc.
$35-45

Sheet Music, "Slumber on Kentucky Babe", lyrics and music by
Freeman and Allemong, published
by Imperial Music Company.
$35-65

MUSIC

Sheet Music, "Sam The Old Accordion Man", 1927, words and music by Walter Donaldson.
$35-65

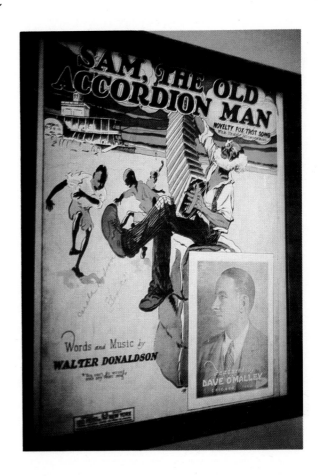

Sheet Music, "They Made It Twice As Nice As Paradise And They Called It Dixieland", lyrics by Raymond Egan, published by Jerome M. Remick & Company.
$35-65

Sheet Music, "The Smiler", by Percy-Wenrich.
$35-65

MUSIC

Sheet Music, "Lena From Palesteena", with Eddie Cantor.
$35-45

Sheet Music, "Mammy's By-Lo Song" words by Ed Marshall, music by Ben Savage.
$35-55

Sheet Music, "Turkey In The Straw", words by Leo Wood, music by Otto Bonnell.
$35-40

TOYS

Jack in the Box type toy with celluloid shrunken head, Japan, 6" (opened).
$30-35

Hard Plastic Walker Toys, Hong Kong, 2 3/4" x 3 3/4".
$15-35 each

Left to Right:
Metal noisemaker, 3 3/4" tall, Japan – **$45-55**
Plastic and wood noisemaker, 7" tall, Japan – **$45-65**
Metal noisemaker, 5 1/2" tall, USA – **$45-65**

Wooden Pull Toy, 8" high x 7" long.
$100-150

TEXTILES

Potholders, 6" x 6½".
$30-35 set

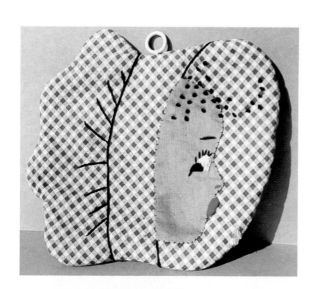

Fabric Potholder, 6" x 6".
$15-25

Potholder, 6" x 6".
$15-25

TEXTILES

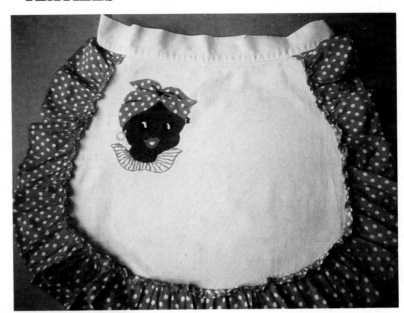

Appliqued Lady on an
Apron, 16½" x 20".
$45-50

Over The Head Apron,
30" x 30".
$45-60

Cross Stitched Tea Towel,
15" x 25½".
$35-40

151

TEXTILES

Three Embroidered Linen
Tea Towels, 12" x 18".
$15-30 each

Cotton Tea Towel, 15" x 26".
$45-60

Cotton Tea Towel, 15" x 45".
$40-45

TEXTILES

Cotton Tea Towel,
16 1/2" x 27 1/2".
$50-70

Cotton Tea Towel,
16 1/2" x 27 1/2".
$45-55

Cotton Tea Towel,
15 1/2" x 26".
$50-65

TEXTILES

Cotton Appliqued Tea Towel.
$35-45

Cotton Square Table Cloth, 51".
$150-190

INDEX